I CHOOSE
to Calm My Anxiety

I CHOOSE SERIES

ELIZABETH
ESTRADA

I CHOOSE
to Calm My Anxiety

Dedicated to Mom and Dad.

ELIZABETH
ESTRADA

I worry and have anxiety.
I often feel **stressed**.
My parents said, "Try to relax,"
But for me that's a **test**.

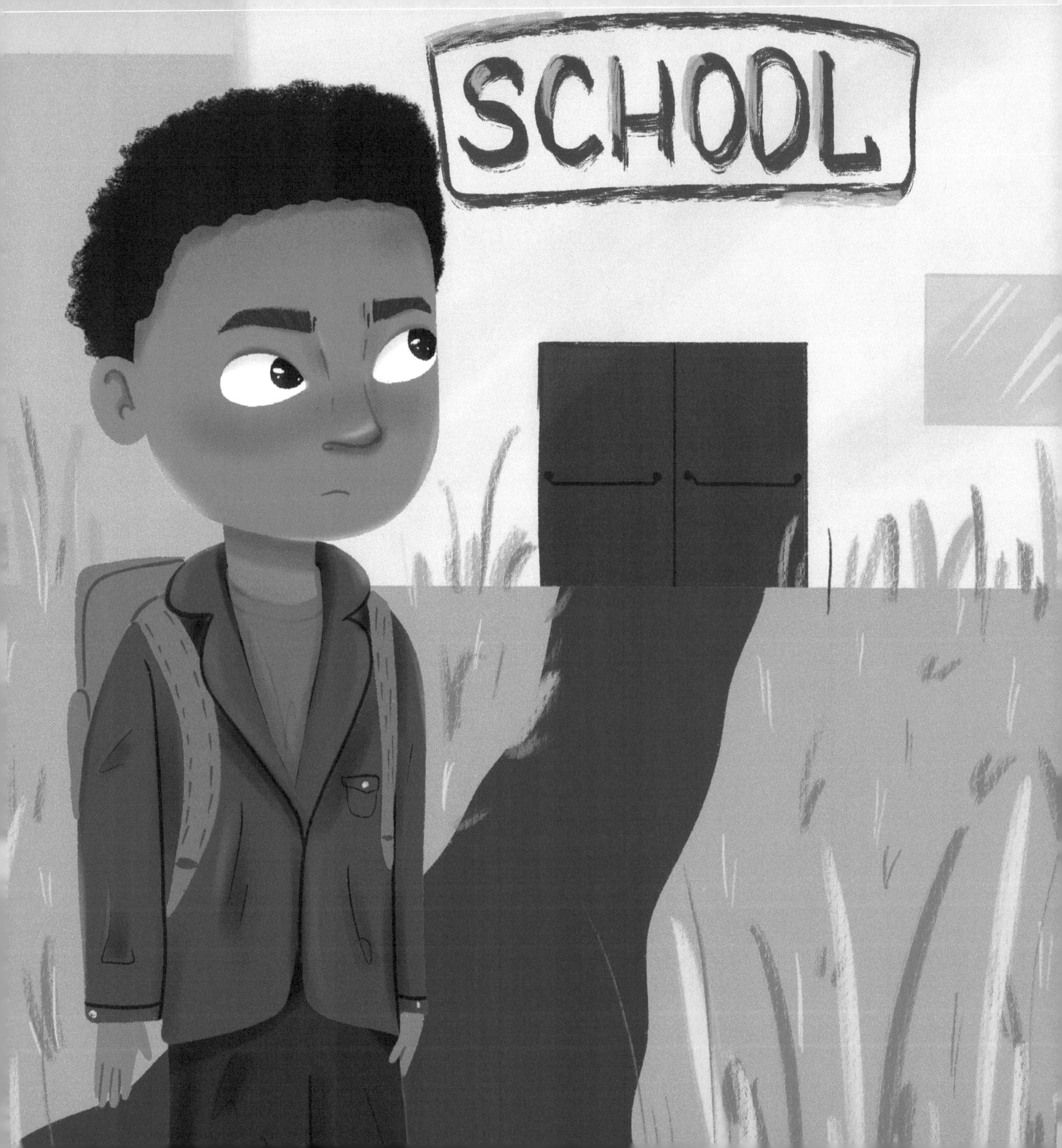
SCHOOL

I worry things won't work out
The way I'd like them **to**.
This makes me very anxious
And scared of what to **do**.

If I have to play a sport
Or learn something new at **school**,
I'd worry that I'd likely fail,
And then look like a **fool**.

Even though I train hard
And practice every **day**,
I can't build up the tools
To push the stress **away**.

My friends said, "What's wrong with you?.
You might need to **change**.
Why do you worry all the time?
We find you very **strange**."

I know I have anxiety,
But calm it I would **try**.
I worried all the time.
I really did not know **why**.

I tried thinking happy thoughts
About places that I **liked**,
And fun things that I loved to do
Like riding on my **bike**.

My best friend, Aiden, talked to me
To try to find the **cause**.
What made me so anxious?
I wondered if I had some **flaws**.

He assured me, "Anxiety is normal.
Everyone experiences it from time to **time**,
But there are strategies that exist
That will help the worry **decline**."

"I will share with you some tools.
You can try using positive **statements**.
'Focus on what I can control' or
'Everything will be okay' are the **greatest**."

"We all have a negative voice
That makes us **worry**.
Choose to listen to your positive voice,
And negativity will soon **scurry**."

"Take some deep breaths,
Then blow with all your **might**,
Making all the stress melt away
Like dandelions in **flight**."

I tried practicing what I learned,
And put it to the ultimate **test**
Whenever something worried me,
Or whenever I felt **stressed**.

Like when my Mom and Dad divorced.
They both said they were **sorry**,
But I'd get time to spend with both.
They said, "Lucas, please don't **worry**."

"We want you to know it's not your fault.
Adults have our stresses **too**.
We can't live together any more,
But we both still care for **you**."

I wondered where I would live.
Not knowing what to **say**,
I tried my hardest not to cry
When Dad said he'd move **away**.

Sometimes things just happen,
There is nothing we can **do**.
I could only control my reactions,
And choose some strategies I **knew**.

I closed my eyes and took a breath.
Then I said, "Everything will be **okay**."
I let my breath out, slow but strong,
Pretending to blow dandelions **away**.

I felt a bit lighter with less worries
Though I knew I was not **cured**.
My anxiety could be calmed,
Of that I was **assured**.

I choose to calm my anxiety,
And think positive **thoughts**.
I can take deep breaths.
Because I'm the **boss**.

I know we all have challenges,
But I will **overcome**.
I won't let worry spoil my life,
A calm Lucas I can **become**.

What anxiety looks like:

IRRITABILITY

DIZZINESS OR
NUMBNESS

SLEEPINESS OR
INSOMNIA

How to Dandelion Breathe

Sit up and let your spine
grow tall.

Imagine a soft dandelion
flower.

Take a deep breath in
and then blow the air
out slowly, sending the
seeds into the air.

Positive Self Talk

I'M GOING TO BE ALL RIGHT.

FOCUS ON MY POSITIVE THOUGHTS.

JUST FOCUS ON THE THINGS I CAN CONTROL. LET GO OF THE THINGS I CAN'T.

TAKE SLOW, DEEP BREATHS TO CALM MY BODY DOWN.

WORRYING IS NOT GOING TO SOLVE ANY PROBLEMS. WHAT IS SOMETHING POSITIVE I CAN DO?

THINK ABOUT THINGS THAT MAKE ME FEEL HAPPY AND SAFE.

I KNOW WHAT MY ANXIETY IS TRYING TO DO, BUT I WON'T LET IT!

I CHOOSE TO CALM MY ANXIETY.

CPSIA information can be obtained
at www.ICGtesting.com
Printed in the USA
BVHW020147141021
618890BV00004B/285

* 9 7 8 1 6 3 7 3 1 2 0 5 6 *